Danube River Cruise Travel Guide 2024

A Comprehensive Cruise Expedition for New Explorers to Discover the Rich Tapestry of Landscapes, Culinary Delights, Historic Marvels, and Cultural Gems.

CAROLYN J BELL.

Table of Contents

Chapter 1. Introduction

Introduction: Unveiling the Danube's Enchantment

Embarking on a journey along the serpentine ribbon of the Danube, I became engulfed in a tale of liquid history and cultural resonance. The river, like a serpentine storyteller, travels through the heart of Europe, exposing the secrets of ancient civilizations.

As I looked at the Danube's beautiful surface, I couldn't help but feel the gravity of its story. My journey began when the river flirted with the German Black Forest, and as I followed its path, I marveled at the convergence of streams that had seen the rise and fall of empires.

The Danube is more than just a river; it's an expressive poet who carves poetry into the form of valleys, meanders and bends. With each passing kilometer, I glided by pages of history, a living tapestry woven by the hands of time.

While navigating its currents, I came upon the remnants of ancient civilizations, as if the river itself was an archeological guide. Roman ruins grew on its banks, holding firm against the currents of change. The medieval whispers of knights and troubadours lingered in the air as we glided by beautiful castles that once guarded trade routes and legacies.

However, the Danube is not a static museum. It pulsates with life, a vibrant canvas painted by the civilizations that line its beaches. In regions where time seemed to stand still, residents recalled their memories over hearty meals, providing a flavor of the region's culinary tradition that dances on the taste buds.

The river's touch extended beyond the physical, caressing the unseen souls of the nations it crossed. As I cruised, I felt a connection to the soul of Central Europe, with the echoes of music from grand concert halls and laughing booming from riverside cafés.

The Danube revealed its attractiveness in the golden glow of sunset, casting a spell that went beyond the capabilities of a typical traveler. It turned into a journey of self-discovery, a flowing adventure that mirrored the ever-changing beauty along its banks.

So, to explore the Danube is to embark on a personal symphony in which the river's melodies resonate with the pulse of Europe's past, present, and future travel opportunities.

Purpose of the Guide

Exploring the Danube's Rich Tapestry.

This book is more than just a collection of itineraries and practical tips; it's a guide to discovering the soul of a Danube River vacation. Its goal extends beyond navigation, aiming to transform your vacation into an exciting exploration of history, culture, and unforgettable experiences.

As you begin your journey, the guide serves as a knowledgeable companion, providing insights into the

Danube's cultural tapestry. It seeks to connect you with the river's pulse, delving into the historical depths that have shaped the landscapes and communities along its banks.

Beyond technical facts, the book aims to generate a sense of wanderlust, encouraging you to not only observe but also engage with the vivid stories woven into the fabric of the Danube. It aims to distract your attention away from the breathtaking views, encouraging you to discover the complexities of each location, from hidden gems to well-known landmarks.

Practicality meets passion as the guide tackles the details of planning, from selecting the right cruise to enjoying local cuisine. It aims to provide you with the information you need to successfully navigate the Danube's waters, making every bend in the river an opportunity for discovery.

In essence, the goal of this book is to elevate your Danube River excursion from a routine vacation to an exciting journey. It invites you to immerse yourself in the cultural symphony that reverberates along the riverbanks, developing a connection with the history, people, and landscapes that make the Danube a timeless marvel.

Chapter 2. Understanding The Danube

Exploring the Danube's Geographic Tapestry.

The Danube, a lovely thread flowing through the heart of Europe, tells a geographical story with every curve and turn. This renowned river originates in Germany's Black Forest and travels through a diverse range of landscapes, providing a visual feast for the passionate visitor.

As the Danube winds its way through the Bavarian countryside, beautiful hills and valleys cradle its banks, creating a tranquil setting that contrasts with the vibrant energy of nearby cities. Moving southeast, the river becomes a natural barrier, carving through the Austrian Alps with astounding precision, providing panoramic views that captivate both the eye and the imagination.

The trip continues as the Danube meanders through the heart of Vienna, where the urban landscape blends seamlessly with the river's flow. From the beautiful bridges that span its waters to the architectural masterpieces that line its banks, the Danube transforms into a living artwork that reflects the cultural grandeur of the places it connects.

Further downstream, the river reaches the Hungarian plains, a vast expanse that stretches in rhythm with the meadows and vineyards that dot the countryside. The rivers of the Danube provide a sense of continuity by connecting the many terrains it encounters, from Germany's rolling hills to Hungary's flat plains.

The river's journey ends at the Danube Delta, a UNESCO World Heritage Site where its waters dance with the Black Sea. A network of canals and marshes creates a distinct ecosystem, showcasing nature's splendor at the river's final destination.

In essence, the Danube's geographical features are a living tableau, a testament to the river's ability to alter and be impacted by the regions it traverses. As you begin your journey, each length of the Danube reveals a new chapter in its geological history, allowing you to see the beauty of a river that brings life to the heart of Europe.

The Danube River, a liquid record etched across Europe, carries not just water but also the echoes of history. Its banks have seen the rise and fall of empires, invaders' footsteps, and the echoes of old civilizations.

The story begins in the Roman Empire, when the Danube served as the empire's natural frontier, providing liquid security against invading forces. The remnants of Roman forts and archeological treasures around the riverbanks are tangible reminders of a bygone era when the Danube was more than just a waterway; it was a line of power and authority.

As the Middle Ages progressed, the Danube became an important trade route, connecting cultures and promoting economic prosperity. Mighty fortifications and castles carefully positioned along its stream tell stories of territorial conflict and the strategic importance of controlling the river's flow.

The Renaissance and Baroque centuries saw a blossoming of art and culture along the Danube's banks. Magnificent palaces and massive churches, each with its own story of creative brilliance, remain reminders of an era when the river served as a conduit for the exchange of ideas and creativity.

However, the Danube did more than just witness history; it also played an important role in shaping it.

The Ottoman Empire's expansion was marked by conflicts along the river's banks, creating a cultural fusion legacy that still permeates the region today.

In the twentieth century, the Danube was at the crossroads of geopolitical changes. From the Cold War era, when it served as a natural border between East and West, until the fall of the Iron Curtain, the river's currents mirrored the ebb and flow of political tides.

Today, when you ride down the Danube, each bend reveals layers of history. The towns and villages that have sprung up along its banks have the imprints of centuries gone by, providing a tangible connection to the historical fabric that transforms the Danube into a living monument to Europe's rich and complex history.

Diverse Cultural Influences: The Danube's Living Mosaic

The Danube River, with its sinuous journey across Central Europe, serves as a cultural kaleidoscope, reflecting the vibrant hues of the many civilizations that have flourished along its banks. As you begin your journey down this liquid highway, you'll be engulfed in a live tapestry of traditions, art, and rituals.

The Germanic tradition that surrounds the river's origins in the Black Forest sets the tone for the cultural symphony that follows. Timber-framed cities and traces of German folklore create an ambiance that reflects a rich history rooted in the heart of Europe.

Moving southeast into Austria, the Danube flows by Vienna, a city known for classical music, art, and imperial glory. The Habsburg heritage is seen in the opulent palaces, splendid architecture, and the very air, which resonates with Mozart and Strauss' music.

As the river flows into Hungary, a distinctive blend of Magyar customs and Turkish influences emerges. Budapest, with its thermal baths, Ottoman-era architecture, and bustling markets, exemplifies the cultural crossroads where East and West meet along the Danube's winding route.

The Danube does more than just absorb culture; it also generates it. The riverbanks are studded with attractive communities where local artisans make traditional products and folk festivals honor long-standing customs. Each point of stop becomes a platform for regional dances, music, and gourmet delights, allowing passengers to immerse themselves in the Danube's lively culture.

Serbia and Bulgaria contribute chapters to this cultural story, with Orthodox monasteries, traditional music, and local handicrafts adding depth to the Danube's evolving character. The river serves as a unifying force, connecting towns while enabling their unique identities to shine through.

In essence, the Danube is not a passive observer of culture; it is a dynamic force that fosters a sense of unity amid diversity.

As you sail down its currents, you'll find yourself immersed in a never-ending discussion of civilizations, each contributing to the harmonious song that defines the Danube's cultural symphony.

Chapter 3. Plan Your Danube River Cruise

Navigating the Danube: Selecting the Right Cruise

In my hunt for the ultimate Danube River cruise, I discovered that the fun begins long before you board the ship. It's a delicate balance of elements that includes personal preferences, travel style, and the allure of the destinations along the route.

1. Define Your Priorities: Before embarking on my Danube tour, I determined what was most important to me. Was it the cultural immersion in historic cities, the breathtaking scenery, or maybe the culinary experiences? Knowing my requirements helps restrict the number of cruise options available.

2. Cruise Duration and Itinerary: The Danube offers a tapestry of sites, each with its unique charm. I considered how much time I wanted to devote to the trip and which cities or locations I wanted to see. Some cruises focus on a specific spot, while others travel the whole length of the river.

3. River cruises come in a variety of sizes, from small boutique boats to larger ships with more amenities. Based on my preferences, I chose a mid-sized cruise that offered a mix of comfort and personalized experiences. It was like finding a floating mansion that suited my travel style.

4. Seasons have an important role in defining the Danube experience. Spring and summer provide vivid panoramas, while fall provides a tapestry of warm colors. Winter cruises capture the charm of holiday markets. Consideration of the time of year was critical in producing the desired feel.

5. Cruise Lines and Reviews: Research became my trusted companion. Reading reviews, comparing amenities, and researching the reputations of several cruise companies allowed me to make an informed decision. I sought a cruise company that met my criteria for service and authenticity.

In the end, I chose a midsummer vacation that promised a mix of cultural exploration and scenic beauty. The ship's panoramic windows provided a floating vantage point for stunning vistas and old villages. Every aspect of the trip, from eating local delicacies on board to attending guided excursions that brought history to life, was tailored to my preferences.

Choosing the right Danube River tour became an important aspect of planning my holiday. It was more than just a practical decision; it was a deliberate effort toward creating an experience that matched my trip goals, turning the Danube into a liquid canvas on which my journey unfolded.

Planning your Danube River cruise entails a thoughtful evaluation of the best dates to set sail, ensuring a balanced mix of good weather, cultural events, and scenic beauty.

1. Spring Splendor (April to June): As the Danube emerges from winter's embrace, it brings a burst of color to the riverbanks. Cruising during this season allows you to see blossoming scenery, warm temperatures, and fewer visitors. It's an ideal season for nature lovers and those seeking a more peaceful experience.

2. Summer Serenity (July to August): The summer months are particularly appealing, with longer days and a lively atmosphere. Cruise under the warm sun, exploring colorful places and engaging in outdoor activities. Be cautious of increased tourist traffic and consider scheduling excursions ahead of time to reserve your place.

3. Autumn Awe (September to October): As the leaves change color, autumn lights the Danube with a rainbow of warm hues. The weather is pleasant, and the harvest season offers a fresh culinary experience. This period provides a blend of scenic grandeur and excellent sailing conditions.

4. Winter Wonder (November to March): Although less popular for sailing, the Danube has a serene beauty

throughout the winter months. If you like gorgeous Christmas markets and don't mind cooler temperatures, a winter cruise might be an excellent experience. Just be prepared for periodic closures and limited outside activities.

Consider your preferences and aims while planning your Danube River vacation itinerary. Whether it's the bloom of spring, the warmth of summer, the vibrant colors of autumn, or the beauty of winter, each season along the Danube reveals a new chapter of its allure.
Duration and Itinerary Considerations:

Crafting Your Danube Odyssey

A Danube River cruise offers a journey through history, culture, and visual grandeur. When planning your holiday, the duration of your cruise and the well-prepared itinerary will impact the richness of your experience.

Danube Sampler: Seven-Day Exploration

For those with limited time, a week-long cruise provides a tantalizing taste of the Danube's beauty. This itinerary takes you from Passau, Germany to Budapest, Hungary, and highlights key attractions. Marvel at Melk Abbey's baroque splendors, stroll through Vienna's imperial gardens, and relax in Budapest's hot baths. While the trip is short, it provides an excellent introduction to the river's cultural and architectural highlights.

The Grand Danube Expedition: 14 Days of Immersion

A two-week tour allows for a more in-depth exploration of the Danube's diverse landscapes and historical tapestry. This extensive tour, which begins in Nuremberg, Germany, and ends in the Black Sea, visits well-known cities such as Vienna and Budapest as well as lesser-known gems like Bratislava and Belgrade. With more days in the program, you may go on leisurely excursions, discover hidden treasures, and build ties with the local culture.

Enchanting Danube Seasons: Tailored Four-Season Cruises

Consider the Danube's beautiful flow across the seasons. A spring cruise may showcase beautiful riverbank beauty, whilst a summer getaway provides enough sunlight for outdoor activities. Fall offers a tapestry of seasonal colors, whilst a winter trip reveals a different form of beauty with Christmas markets. Tailor your duration and itinerary to match the seasonal charm that best suits your trip preferences.

Whatever length and itinerary you choose, the Danube offers a symphony of experiences. Whether it's a quick overture or a lengthy composition, your river excursion allows you to immerse yourself in the captivating melodies of Europe's cultural center.

7-Day Danube Expedition: A Symphony of Highlights

Day 1–2: Passau, Germany
Begin your journey in Passau, where the Danube, Inn, and Ilz rivers meet.
Explore the lovely Old Town, known for its baroque architecture.
Visit St. Stephen's Cathedral and the stunning Veste Oberhaus Castle.

Day Three: Linz, Austria
Cruise to Linz, a city with a vibrant arts and cultural scene.
Visit the Ars Electronica Center and indulge in Linzer Torte, a local delicacy.
Optional journey to the medieval settlement of Český Krumlov over the Czech border.

Day 4: Melk and Dürnstein.
Sail to Melk and see the stunning Melk Abbey, a UNESCO World Heritage Site.
Continue to Dürnstein, a picturesque hamlet with a castle and cobblestone streets.
Experience a wine-tasting excursion in the Wachau Valley.

Day 5–6: Vienna, Austria
Arrive in Vienna, a place of classical music and imperial splendor.
Explore Schönbrunn Palace, St. Stephen's Cathedral, and Belvedere Palace.
A truly Viennese experience involves attending a classical symphony or opera.

Day Seven: Budapest, Hungary.
End your tour in Budapest, a city divided by the Danube.
Visit Buda Castle, Fisherman's Bastion, and soak in the thermal waters.
Optional evening cruise offers sweeping views of Budapest's illuminated landmarks.

14-Day Danube Immersion: Uncovering Hidden Treasures

Day 1–3: Nuremberg, Germany
Begin your lengthy journey at Nuremberg, known for its medieval buildings.
Discover the Old Town, Nuremberg Castle, and the Documentation Centre.
Visit the Nazi Party Rally Grounds and Courtroom 600, the site of the Nuremberg Trials.

Day 4–5: Regensburg and Passau
Cruise to Regensburg, a UNESCO World Heritage site with well-preserved medieval structures.

Continue to Passau, where you may see the baroque architecture and have a lovely promenade along the river.

Day Six: Linz, Austria
Spend the day in Linz, delving deeper into its cultural offerings.
Visit the Lentos Art Museum and the Brucknerhaus performing space.

Day 7: Dürnstein and Melk.
Return to Dürnstein for a more leisurely exploration of the vineyards and history.
Return to Melk Abbey for an in-depth exploration of its art and architecture.

Day 8–9: Vienna, Austria
Spend more time in Vienna to immerse yourself in its culture.
Explore lesser-known districts, visit local markets, and try authentic Viennese cuisine.

Day 10–11: Bratislava, Slovakia
Cruise to Bratislava, a city rich in history and beauty.
Explore Bratislava Castle, walk around the Old Town, and savor Slovakian delicacies.

Day 12–14: Budapest, Hungary
End your immersive adventure in Budapest.
Explore off-the-beaten-path locations, visit the Hungarian National Museum, and sample local cuisine.

Spend your last day with a relaxing spa treatment and a farewell dinner overlooking the Danube.

Chapter 4. Exploring the Danube's Landscape

scenic views and natural wonders

Cruising down the Danube is more than just a tour of history and culture; it's a visual feast of breathtaking landscapes and natural wonders that leave an indelible impression. As the river meanders across various landscapes, each bend reveals a new chapter in the story of Europe's natural beauty.

One of the most remarkable features is the Wachau Valley, which surrounds the river with rolling hills covered with vineyards and dotted with lovely settlements. The vine-clad hills create a patchwork quilt of greenery, and medieval settlements like Dürnstein seem like time capsules nestled against this stunning backdrop. I remember standing on the terrace, watching the sun cast a golden glow over the valley, and feeling as if I had stepped into a painting.

As we cruise over the Austrian Alps, the landscape transforms into a stunning symphony of peaks and valleys. The chilly mountain air, snow-capped peaks, and mirror-like reflections in the river produced a peaceful atmosphere. It was a time of complete tranquility, a connection with nature's beauty that left an indelible mark on my soul.

As we traveled through the Danube Delta towards the Black Sea, the environment changed dramatically. The delta is a vibrant patchwork of canals, marshes, and reed beds teeming with wildlife. Flocks of birds passed above, and the rustling reeds created a soothing sound. Exploring this strange ecosystem seemed like entering a timeless world where nature governed the cycle of life.

The Iron Gates, a little valley between Serbia and Romania, proved to be an unexpected joy. The towering cliffs built by the river over millennia generated a sense of awe. The journey through this natural gem seemed like a movie adventure, with each twist and turn revealing new layers of the raw beauty that surrounded the Danube.

These meetings highlighted the Danube's role as a conduit for not just human history, but also the forces that shaped the nation itself. The breathtaking panoramas and natural wonders along the river are more than just sights to see; they are moments of connection with the Earth's beauty, reminders of the delicate dance between water and land that has played out over millennia along the Danube's meandering course.

Unique Flora and Fauna

The Danube River, known for its cultural and historical tapestry, also reveals a diverse flora and fauna along its banks. During my own Danube River tour, seeing this unique ecosystem added an unexpected level of enchantment to the journey.

Flora: The Riverside Symphony

As the ship entered the Wachau Valley, the hillsides burst into bloom. Vineyards cascaded down the slopes, their leaves catching the sunlight in hues of green and gold. Wildflowers bordered the riverbanks, creating a kaleidoscope of colors that flowed through the air. Apricots and apple orchards filled the air with their aroma, adding to the sensory delight of the journey.

One particularly memorable experience was a guided nature walk in Austria when our party followed a riverside path. The guide showed us the local plants, explaining their medicinal uses and cultural significance. We encountered exquisite wild orchids and strong alpine meadowfoam blooms, all contributing to the biological symphony that mirrored the Danube's movement.

Another highlight was a visit to the Danube Delta, where the river flows into the Black Sea. The wetlands are alive with aquatic vegetation, reeds, and water lilies. It was like entering into a watercolor painting, with each natural stroke creating a beauty of biodiversity.

Fauna: Wildlife on the banks

As the expedition progressed, the Danube revealed its hidden inhabitants. Birds of prey flew above, their keen eyes searching for fish in the river. Swans sailed swiftly along the river, while ducks and herons sought refuge in quiet corners. The banks were alive with the sounds of songbirds, giving a natural soundtrack to our journey.

During a beach trip in the Danube Delta, our little boat navigated through narrow tunnels and reed-lined waterways. It was here that we encountered the diverse bird life that inhabits the delta. From gorgeous egrets to colorful kingfishers, the trip was a birdwatcher's dream.

Amid gorgeous castles and historic cities, the presence of the Danube's nature and animals provided moments of tranquility. One evening, as the sun set, I found myself on the ship's deck, watching a family of swans soar by. It was a simple but profound moment, a reminder that the river's ecology continued to dance even as humans did.

In essence, the unique flora and animals along the Danube added a layer of natural poetry to the river's cultural and historical epic. It served as a reminder that, underneath the architectural marvels and fabled cities, the Danube is a living creature with its own story to tell—one written in the language of leaves, flowers, and the gentle rustling of riverbank reeds.

Outdoor activities along the riverbank

Hiking in the Scenic Wachau Valley is a nature lover's paradise.

The Wachau Valley, located along the banks of the Danube between Melk and Krems in Austria, greets hikers with breathtaking views and charming vineyards. A trekking adventure in the Wachau Valley is a journey into a world of terraced vines, medieval castles, and charming villages that unroll like chapters from a story.

Key highlights:

1. Dürnstein to Krems trail:
Begin your visit to the medieval hamlet of Dürnstein, known for its castle ruins and historic beauty.
Hike along well-marked pathways to Krems, with stunning views of the Danube and the surrounding vine-covered hills.
Pass through apricot orchards and tiny wine villages to immerse yourself in the region's agricultural bounty.

2. Vineyard panoramas:
Explore the terraced vineyards that blanket the slopes, producing a visual feast of tidy rows of grapevines against the backdrop of the river.
Visit local wineries along the way to sample wines and learn about traditional winemaking techniques.

3. Ruins of Castle Dürnstein
Take a detour to see the remnants of Castle Dürnstein, which sits high above the town.
Enjoy magnificent views of the Danube Valley from the castle's high point, making it a great spot for rest and reflection.

4. Krems' Old Town Exploration:
End your adventure at Krems, which is a well-preserved medieval old town.
Wander through cobblestone alleys, discover historic residences, and relax at one of the local cafés to experience the unique atmosphere.

Tips for Hikers:

Trail Difficulty: The hiking paths in the Wachau Valley cater to a wide range of fitness levels. Choose pathways that correspond to your hiking ability and endurance.
Seasonal Considerations: Spring and autumn provide comfortable weather and picturesque scenery. Summer might be warmer, which is ideal for those who like extended daylight hours. Winter hikes are doable, however trail conditions may vary.

Wear sturdy hiking shoes, especially if exploring dirt trails in vineyards or steep areas.

Hiking in the Wachau Valley is more than just a physical adventure; it's an entire experience that connects you to the natural beauty and cultural richness of this well-known Austrian region.

Kayaking or canoeing on the Danube provides a unique and intimate perspective on this famous river, allowing enthusiasts to immerse themselves in its natural beauty and cultural richness. Here's a snapshot of the experience:

1. Tranquil waters and scenic beauty:
Paddling along the Danube provides a relaxing and tranquil experience as you navigate its quiet waters.

The riverbanks grow with breathtaking vistas, vineyards, tiny villages, and lush vegetation.

2. Flexibility of exploration:
Kayaking or canoeing provides you with freedom of exploration, enabling you to visit remote areas and quiet coves that are off the beaten path.
Navigate at your own pace, choose whether to float along slowly or pick up the pace for a little excitement.

3. Close Encounters With Nature:
Glide softly over the water, giving you the opportunity for close encounters with the many wildlife along the riverbanks.
Birdwatching gets exciting when you see herons, swans, and other waterfowl in their natural habitat.

4. Historical and cultural perspectives:
The Danube is home to many historical sites and monuments, and kayaking or canoeing provides a unique perspective from which to view these buildings.
Paddle past ancient castles, riverside fortresses, and gorgeous villages that tell tales from the past.

5. Adventure and Relaxation Combined:
While the Danube offers a calm kayaking experience, there are also sections with minor rapids for those who like a little more excitement.
Enjoy the combination of vigorous exploration and the serenity of drifting with the currents.

6. Multi Day Expeditions:
For the adventurous at heart, multi-day kayaking or canoeing experiences are available, allowing you to see more of the Danube's sceneries.
Camping by the riverbanks under the starry sky lends a sense of adventure to the trip.

7. Locally Guided Tours:
Local outfitters generally provide guided kayaking or canoeing experiences that give insights into the area's history, culture, and nature.
Experienced guides may enhance your journey by sharing stories and pointing out hidden gems along the way.

Kayaking or canoeing on the Danube is more than just a physical activity; it's an immersive experience that combines natural adventure with cultural exploration, providing a unique perspective on this old and beautiful river.

Birdwatching along the Danube Riverbanks is an exciting experience, allowing visitors to see a variety of bird species in their natural habitat. The riverbanks provide a haven for a variety of animals, from the graceful swans to the agile herons and cormorants. During a stroll or sail, one may see these flying inhabitants, adding to the natural beauty of the area. Birdwatchers may also encounter migratory species, adding seasonal diversity to the bird show along the Danube.

The presence of songbirds is especially noticeable, filling the air with wonderful sounds as they flit among the trees and reeds. Riverside towns and natural reserves along the Danube offer ideal vantage points for birdwatching, creating a tranquil environment in which enthusiasts may observe, identify, and appreciate diverse species. The many habitats along the riverbanks create a dynamic ambiance, making birding a rewarding and peaceful outdoor activity for anybody looking to connect with nature during their Danube River journey.

Golfing with panoramic river views

Golf enthusiasts may enjoy a one-of-a-kind and breathtaking experience along the Danube, with the serene beauty of the riverbanks serving as the backdrop for a round of golf. Imagine teeing off against the lush greens, with the beautiful river running in the background, providing a scene that combines the precision of the sport with the tranquility of nature.

Several golf courses near the Danube provide not only challenging fairways but also breathtaking views of the river and surrounding landscape. These courses, designed to make use of the natural terrain, provide players with an immersive experience that goes beyond the game itself.

As you swing through your round, the rhythmic flow of the Danube serves as a nice backdrop. The courses often mix the contours of the terrain, providing vantage points for players to pause, soak in the scenery, and appreciate the unique allure of playing amid such natural beauty.

The fairways provide views of riverside communities, historic buildings, and, depending on the time of day, the changing colors of the sky reflected in the water. Whether you're a seasoned or casual golfer, the combination of sport and environment along the Danube lends a sense of peace and joy to the game.

It's more than just a game of precision and talent; it's an opportunity to immerse yourself in the Danube's visual majesty, with each swing contributing to the larger symphony that the river creates as it flows through the landscapes it graces.

Engaging in yoga or meditation by the Danube River is a peaceful and rejuvenating experience that combines natural settings with concentrated exercises. The steady flow of the river and the tranquil environment provide an ideal setting for those seeking moments of inner serenity and meditation.

1. Riverside yoga sessions:
Yoga by the Danube typically involves setting up mats or practicing on grassy riverbanks.
The rhythmic sounds of running water provide a relaxing accompaniment to yoga poses and stretches.
Instructors guide participants through various poses, helping them connect with nature and themselves.

2. Meditation in Nature:
Finding a serene area beside the river, folks may meditate on the soothing symphony of nature.
The gentle breeze, the murmur of water, and the rustle of leaves create a tranquil atmosphere.

Practitioners often focus on mindfulness, breathing, and grounding exercises to connect with the present moment.

3. Sunrise and Sunset Sessions:
Many people choose to practice yoga or meditation during the beautiful hours of dawn or sunset.
The exquisite hues painted on the sky and the reflection on the lake add to the experience, creating a tranquil atmosphere.
This provides a pleasant start or end to the day, instilling a sense of balance and thanks.

4. Group Retreats & Workshops:
Some Danube venues conduct group yoga retreats or courses that combine practice and wellness activities.
Experienced instructors lead participants through programs that address both physical postures and mental well-being.

5. Connection to Nature:
Practicing yoga or meditation by the river allows people to connect with nature and find comfort in the simplicity of the surroundings.
The openness of the riverbanks and expansive views contribute to a sense of spaciousness and tranquility.

6. Accessible at All Levels:
Yoga or meditation by the Danube is suitable for people of all skill levels, whether they are experienced practitioners or beginners.

The natural setting allows people to go at their own pace, fostering a non-competitive and friendly attitude.

In essence, yoga or meditation by the Danube provides a full experience that combines the benefits of consciousness with the healing properties of nature. It's an opportunity to nurture the body, mind, and spirit in an atmosphere that seamlessly blends the beauty of the river with the quest for inner serenity.

Fishing for local species on the Danube.

Fishing along the Danube is more than just a recreational activity; it also allows you to interact with the river's diverse aquatic ecology. Whether you're an experienced fisherman or a novice, the Danube's waters provide an enticing environment in which to throw your line and immerse yourself in the local fishing culture.

Key Aspects:

1. Diverse fish species:
The Danube is home to a diverse range of fish species, including carp, catfish, perch, and pike.
Anglers might target certain species depending on the place and time of year.

2. Scenic fishing spots:

Riverside towns and villages typically have designated fishing areas, which provide a lovely backdrop for fishers.

The tranquil backwaters and meandering lengths offer ideal conditions for a relaxing fishing experience.

3. Local Fishing Culture:

Engaging with local fishermen and fishing villages adds cultural depth to the experience.

Learning about traditional fishing strategies and techniques may deepen your appreciation for the region's heritage.

4. Catch-and-release practices:

To protect the environment, several Danube areas promote catch-and-release practices.

Understanding local laws promotes responsible fishing and helps conservation efforts.

5. Guided fishing excursions:

Opting for guided fishing trips led by local professionals enhances the whole experience.

Guides not only provide valuable insights into the best fishing spots, but they also share stories about the river's history and the significance of particular fish species.

6. Seasonal variations:

Fish behavior is influenced by seasonal changes in fishing conditions.

Spring and early summer may be ideal seasons for some species, although autumn gives a variety of alternatives.

7. Equipment and techniques:
Tailor your fishing gear to the specific species you're after.
Changing your strategy, whether it's fly fishing for trout or using bait for catfish, increases your chances of landing a solid catch.

8. Relaxation and Connection:
Fishing by the Danube provides a peaceful and contemplative experience.
Whether it is a solo effort or a group activity, it provides a unique chance to engage with the natural beauty of the river.

Remember to check local regulations, get the necessary licenses, and use sustainable fishing practices to ensure a harmonious coexistence with the Danube's aquatic biodiversity.

Horseback Riding Near River Towns

An Equestrian Adventure

Immerse yourself in the breathtaking scenery along the Danube by going horseback riding through the beautiful river villages. This outdoor activity provides a new perspective, allowing you to travel beautiful routes, enjoy the tranquility of the countryside, and see the grandeur of the Danube from a different angle.

Key experiences:

1. Riverside pathways: Follow meandering paths through river towns for views of stunning architecture, lush meadows, and the tranquil flow of the Danube.

2. Countryside Exploration: Explore the surrounding countryside to discover hidden gems that other techniques may not reveal. Horseback riding provides a sense of freedom and a deeper connection to nature.

3. Historical Sites: Ride to historical sites located near river towns. Discover historic castles, rural villages, and monuments that tell tales about the region's rich history.

4. Panoramic Views: Climb to high elevations for breathtaking panoramic views of the Danube. Enjoy the tranquility as you gaze at the river's gentle flow and the surrounding surroundings.

5. Local Culture: Connect with the local equestrian community and learn about the cultural significance of horseback riding in the region. Some localities may provide guided rides with educated inhabitants.

6. Vineyard Excursions: In wine-producing regions, mount up for rides through vineyards with rows of grapevines providing a lovely backdrop. Some vacations also involve visits to nearby wineries for sampling.

7. Sunset Rides: Take sunset rides along the riverbanks, where the changing colors of the sky provide a wonderful light over the Danube. It's a relaxing and romantic way to end a day of exploration.

Practical tips:

Make sure you choose a reputable horseback riding outfitter with well-trained horses and experienced guides.
Wear appropriate riding gear, such as comfortable clothes and closed-toe shoes.
Check the path's difficulty level to ensure that it is appropriate for your riding abilities.
Follow the safety instructions provided by the outfitter to ensure a safe and enjoyable excursion.

Horseback riding near river towns along the Danube is more than just a recreational sport; it's a journey that allows you to connect with nature, absorb local culture, and create lasting memories against the backdrop of this well-known European waterway.

Chapter 5: Danube Culinary Delights

A Danube River cruise is more than just a tour of history and beauty; it's also a culinary excursion that urges you to try the many specialties of the regions that border the riverbanks. Every bend of the Danube introduces you to different culinary traditions, exciting your taste buds with a symphony of regional specialties.

1. Gastronomic Delights of Germany:
Begin your German culinary journey with hearty sausages, pretzels, and sauerkraut.
Enjoy Bavarian delights such as Schweinshaxe (roasted pork knuckle) and Weisswurst (white sausage).
Dive into the beer culture with a variety of local brews, ranging from crisp lagers to robust bocks.

2. Culinary elegance in Austria:
Try the famous Wiener Schnitzel, a breaded and fried veal or pork cutlet from Austria.
Satisfy your sweet craving with Sachertorte, a wonderful chocolate cake, and Apfelstrudel, a classic apple pastry.
Pair your meals with renowned Austrian wines that reflect the region's vineyard quality.

3. Extravaganza of Hungarian spices:
Enjoy the bold flavors of Hungarian cuisine with dishes like Goulash, a thick and delicious stew.

Try the original Lángos, which are deep-fried flatbreads topped with sour cream and cheese.
Visit spice stores and try paprika-infused foods, which are common in Hungarian cuisine.

4. Slovakian Culinary Treasures:
Try Haluky, Slovakia's equivalent of gnocchi, which is often served with sheep cheese and bacon.
Indulge in hearty bean and sausage soups inspired by the country's rural cooking traditions.
Try local dairy products like bryndza cheese, which is used in many Slovakian dishes.

5. Serbian Savory Dishes:
Dive into Serbian cuisine with evapi, which are grilled minced beef kebabs often served with flatbread.
Enjoy the unique flavors of Ajvar, a peppery spice, and Kajmak, a creamy dairy spread.
Quench your thirst with Rakija, a fruit brandy popular across the Balkans.

6. Culinary surprises in Romania:
Try Mămăligă, a traditional Romanian polenta that is often served with sour cream and cheese.
Try Mici, a classic street snack made of grilled sausages seasoned with garlic and spices.
Finish with Papanasi, a delicious dessert made with fried doughnuts, sour cream, and jam.

7. Culinary traditions in Bulgaria:

Banitsa, a Bulgarian pastry loaded with cheese and eggs that exemplifies the country's baking skills, is a must-try.

Try Kavarma, a slow-cooked stew including a variety of meats and vegetables.

Try the Shopska Salad, a tasty mix of tomatoes, cucumbers, peppers, and feta.

Allow your taste buds to guide you as you sail down the Danube, allowing the river's gourmet symphony to wow you with a delectable array of regional specialties and authentic flavors.

Popular regional dishes.

Austrian Wiener Schnitzel is a culinary classic.

Wiener Schnitzel is an Austrian culinary classic whose simple but delicious recipe transcends borders. This classic veal-based dish has a tenderized and breaded cutlet that is pan-fried to golden perfection. As a result, the crispy, golden exterior protects the luscious, delectable flesh within.

Elements to consider:

Veal Cutlet: The classic Wiener Schnitzel is made from pounded veal to a thin, uniform thickness. Variations with pork or chicken are also popular.

Breading Method: First, the cutlet is coated in flour, then in beaten eggs, and last in breadcrumbs. The dish's distinctive texture is complemented by the extensive breading procedure.

Pan-frying: Cook the cutlet in clarified butter or oil until golden brown. This method of grilling produces a crispy top while leaving the meat tender.

Wiener Schnitzel is often served with a slice of lemon and a side of potato salad or parsley potatoes. The lemon's acidic flavor provides a nice contrast to the dish's richness.

Wiener Schnitzel has a unique place in Austrian cuisine because it epitomizes the ideal balance of simplicity and sophistication. It's more than just a meal; it's a cultural experience that has left its imprint on dining tables all over the world, enabling everyone to enjoy Austria's culinary heritage.

Austrian Sachertorte: A Chocolate Delight.

Sachertorte, a typical Austrian food, is recognized for its rich and luscious chocolate flavor. This famous Vienna cake consists of layers of delicious chocolate cake separated by a thin layer of apricot jam. Each slice is coated in a glossy, dark chocolate glaze, adding a touch of elegance. Sachertorte has become a symbol of Austrian patisserie talent and a must-try for visitors to the country's culinary delights, often served with a dollop of unsweetened whipped cream.

Hungarian goulash: A hearty Hungarian classic.

Goulash, a classic Hungarian stew, is a thick and flavorful dish with global appeal. Goulash is a culinary masterpiece made from soft chunks of meat, usually beef, slow-cooked with onions, paprika, and a variety of spices.

This powerful dish often incorporates potatoes, carrots, and bell peppers, yielding a savory and cozy meal. Goulash, typically prepared over an open flame in a cauldron, captures the essence of Hungarian culinary traditions, providing a sense of coziness and robust flavors.

Goulash, whether eaten in Budapest's bustling markets or quiet rural taverns, exemplifies Hungary's dedication to culinary excellence and the art of slow cooking. Goulash is a symbol of Hungarian hospitality and a must-try for anybody exploring Danube cuisine, owing to its rich aroma and distinct flavor.

Lángos: A Hungarian Deep-Fried Delight.

Lángos is a popular Hungarian street food with a crispy outside and soft, doughy inside. This delectable treat begins with a simple dough of wheat, water, yeast, and salt. After rising, the dough is stretched to a thin, flat shape and deep-fried till golden brown.

Lángos, which is often served hot and fresh, may be consumed in several ways. It is frequently topped with a thick layer of sour cream and shredded cheese, giving it a rich and creamy texture. Toppings such as garlic, garlic butter, or a sprinkle of salt may be added for additional flavor.

Lángos is a versatile dish, and although the original version remains popular, new variations using toppings like ham, bacon, and even Nutella have gained popularity. Lángos epitomizes the wonderful simplicity of Hungarian cuisine, whether served as a snack at a local market or as a substantial street food option.

Haluky (Slovakia): A Delicious Culinary Tradition.

Haluky, a traditional Slovakian meal, is a hearty and comforting supper that showcases the country's rich culinary heritage. The irregular, gnocchi-like shapes of these dumplings, made from grated potatoes and flour, distinguish them. Haluky are known for their superb chewiness and rustic texture after being boiled and pan-fried.

Bryndzové Haluky is one of the most popular variants, with the dumplings liberally coated with bryndza, a sour sheep cheese unique to the region. The dish is sometimes served with smoked bacon or sausage, which adds a delightful richness to the flavor profile.

Haluky has a special place in Slovakian households, and it is often served during family gatherings, holidays, and cultural events. Its simple yet satisfying nature embodies the essence of traditional Slovakian comfort food, offering a wonderful and authentic taste of the country's culinary heritage.

cevapi (Serbia), a Balkan delight.

Evapi, a well-known Serbian dish, exemplifies the region's diverse flavors. These little, grilled minced beef sausages are a Serbian culinary delicacy, known for their savory taste and distinctive technique. Evapi are shaped into finger-sized cylinders before grilling and are often made from a variety of ground meats—often a combination of beef and pork—seasoned with garlic, onions, and other spices. This dish is a delicious combination of smoky, grilled deliciousness and rich, savory accompaniments, served with somun (a kind of flatbread), chopped onions, and a dollop of kajmak (a creamy dairy spread). Evapi is a culinary experience that captures the essence of Serbian hospitality and gastronomic tradition, whether eaten as street food or as part of a complete meal.

Cornmeal Treat from Mămăligă, Romania

Mămăligă is a traditional Romanian dish that has a significant place in the country's culinary heritage. Mămăligă, sometimes called Romanian polenta, is made from coarse yellow cornmeal, water, and salt. The mixture is cooked until it thickens and resembles porridge.

This customizable dinner may be served in several ways:

1. Mămăligă is often served as a side dish with stews, grilled meats, and sausages. Its delicate flavor contrasts nicely with more robust main courses.

2. Mămăligă may sometimes take center stage as a major dish. Layer it with cheese, sour cream, or butter for a delicious and warm dinner.

3. Sweet Variations: Mămăligă may be sweetened with sugar and topped with fruits, jams, or honey for a sweet dessert. This sweet variant is enjoyed as a dessert or for breakfast.

4. Grilled Mămăligă: Grilling slices of Mămăligă adds a delicious smokiness and a crispy skin, giving this traditional dish a unique twist.

Mămăligă is a cultural symbol as well as a culinary delight, representing the simplicity and ingenuity of Romanian cuisine. Its modest components belie the rich and calming sensation it gives, making it a popular choice on Romanian menus and a must-try for travelers exploring the region's distinct flavors.

Bulgarian Banitsa - A Flaky Pastry Tradition

Banitsa, a classic Bulgarian pastry, has become a symbol of the country's culinary heritage. This traditional dessert is made by stacking thin filo pastry sheets with a combination of whisked eggs, Bulgarian feta cheese (sirene), and sometimes yogurt. The layers are then fried till brown, resulting in a savory and tasty pastry.

Banitsa may be prepared in several ways to accommodate varied tastes and settings. Spinach, leeks, and minced meat are sometimes added to enhance the flavor profile. The dish is often offered at special occasions, family gatherings, or as a beloved breakfast item when paired with a dollop of yogurt.

Banitsa's delicious taste, along with its cultural significance, has made it a Bulgarian table staple. The lunch demonstrates the country's commitment to preserving culinary traditions while also delivering a delightful insight into Bulgarian hospitality and cuisine.

Schweinshaxe (Germany) is a pork lovers' paradise.

Schweinshaxe is a classic German dish, particularly popular in Bavaria. This exquisite delicacy, made with a roasted ham hock, demonstrates German pork culinary prowess. The crispy, crackling skin on the outside and the tender, succulent flesh on the inside set this dinner apart.

To increase the richness of the pork in Schweinshaxe, the ham hock is often marinated or rubbed with a spice combination that includes garlic, caraway, and, on rare occasions, beer. The hock is slow-cooked until the meat is soft and the skin is perfectly crispy.

Schweinshaxe is often served as a strong main dish with traditional accompaniments like sauerkraut and potato dumplings. This dish is popular among those searching for a true flavor of German cuisine, especially in Bavaria's cozy beer gardens and traditional pubs, because it combines crispy skin, tasty meat, and aromatic spices.

Weisswurst is a Bavarian delicacy.

Weisswurst, or "white sausage," is a traditional Bavarian delicacy and a culinary symbol of Germany. This mild, white sausage is made with minced veal and back bacon and seasoned with fresh parsley, mace, onions, ginger, and cardamom. The sausages, which are enclosed in a thin membrane, are boiled rather than grilled or fried to preserve their delicate flavor and ensure a smooth texture.

Weisswurst is a beautifully cooked sausage that is often served in the middle of the morning, making it a Bavarian breakfast or brunch classic. They are often served with sweet mustard, pretzels, and a refreshing Weissbier (white beer).

Weisswurst is culturally significant in Bavaria, and eating it is a custom; the sausages are often had before lunchtime. This culinary treasure not only illustrates Bavaria's commitment to its gastronomic heritage, but also provides an excellent culinary experience for visitors exploring German cuisine along the Danube's banks.

Serbian Rakija: A Spirited Tradition

Rakija, a traditional Serbian beverage, is a potent fruit brandy with strong roots in the country's culinary and cultural heritage. This powerful drink has traditionally been made by distilling various fruits, including plums (ljivovica), apricots, grapes, and more.

Rakija, with an alcohol content ranging from 40% to 60%, is often shipped during special occasions, family gatherings, and celebrations. Its creation is a communal event in which families and communities work together to make and share this precious elixir.

Each location in Serbia is proud of its distinct Rakija recipe, resulting in a diverse spectrum of flavors. Rakija, whether served as an aperitif or for toasting, epitomizes Serbian hospitality's warmth and conviviality. It is more than just a drink; it symbolizes fraternity, tradition, and the spirit of Serbian culture.

Papanasi (Romania): A delicious Romanian dessert.

Papanasi are traditional Romanian doughnuts that play an important role in the country's cuisine. These delicious treats are made using cottage cheese, flour, eggs, and a touch of vanilla. The dough is shaped into little, spherical dumplings with a center depression that holds various toppings.

Papanas are often served warm and topped with a generous dollop of sour cream and fruit jam, which is sometimes made from berries such as sour cherries or raspberries. Papanasi is a famous dessert in Romania, where it is enjoyed on several occasions and festivals. Papanasi embodies the rich and beautiful flavors of Romanian cuisine, whether served as a warm delicacy or a stunning dessert.

Kavarma (Bulgaria): A Harmonic Culinary Journey

Kavarma, a traditional Bulgarian meal, is a slow-cooked stew that highlights the region's diverse flavors and customs. Kavarma is a delicious dish that is often prepared with a variety of meats such as pork, chicken, or lamb.

The meats are marinated in a variety of spices, including garlic, paprika, and herbs, which give the feast layers of taste. Tomatoes, peppers, and onions provide freshness and sweetness to the stew, resulting in a harmonious balance of tastes.

The method of preparation differentiates Kavarma. Slow-cooking marinated meats and vegetables enables the flavors to combine and intensify. This gentle cooking procedure results in delicate, succulent meats enveloped by a robust and aromatic sauce.

Kavarma is often served boiling, with rice or crusty bread to soak up the rich juices. The dinner not only feeds the stomach but also gives a glimpse into Bulgaria's culinary heritage, where the unhurried cooking method transforms simple ingredients into a symphony of flavors that appeal to both locals and visitors.

Mici (Romania): Perfectly grilled.

Mici, also known as "mititei," is a traditional Romanian dish that is enjoyed by both locals and visitors. These little, grilled sausages are a gourmet delight rich in flavor and tradition. Mici, which are often made from a variety of minced meats (typically pig, cow, and lamb), demonstrate Romania's ability to make delicious, well-seasoned grilled meats.

Mici's distinct taste is obtained with a precise combination of garlic, black pepper, and other spices. The sausages are compressed into cylindrical forms before being fried to perfection. As a result, the dish has a crispy outside and a juicy, delicious inside.

Mici are often served in a relaxed, communal setting, making them ideal for parties, festivals, and family picnics. Mici epitomizes the essence of Romanian cuisine—a delightful combination of simplicity, rich flavors, and communal dining—served with mustard, fresh bread, and, on occasion, pickles or fries.

Cruise Dining Recommendations

A Danube River cruise is more than just a beautiful excursion; it's also a culinary adventure set against the backdrop of Europe's cultural treasures. Here are some dining options to help you enjoy every moment of your cruise:

1. Gastronomic Delights On Board:
- Dine in the cruise ship's different restaurants, which provide a mix of foreign and regional cuisine.
- Attend themed dining events that showcase the culinary pleasures of the Danube's many civilizations.

2. Tastes of Local Cuisine:
- Take advantage of onboard sampling to get familiar with the cuisines of each location. As part of the entire experience, try local wines, cheeses, and delicacies.

3. Dining outside on the deck:
- Dine on the outdoor deck while admiring the panoramic views as you pass through charming cities and breathtaking scenery.

4. Specialty dining experiences:
- Attend one-of-a-kind dining events, such as a sunset dinner or a barbecue night on the terrace. These interactions provide a mystical element to your culinary journey.

5. Explore Local Restaurants:
- During port breaks, visit the towns along the Danube to try authentic local cuisine. Your cruise operator may provide guided culinary excursions and restaurant recommendations.

6. Workshops and demonstrations in the kitchen.
- Take part in culinary lessons or demonstrations led by local chefs onboard. Learn how to create traditional dishes and bring home a taste of your Danube experience.

7. Dietary Preferences Customized
- Inform the cruise staff ahead of time if you have any culinary preferences or constraints. Most cruise lines are accommodating and may adjust meals to meet particular needs.

8. Options for casual and fine dining:
- Have the best of both worlds by combining informal and elegant dining. Casual dining options offer a relaxed atmosphere for more formal occasions, whilst fine dining evenings provide an amazing setting for more formal functions.

9. Celebratory dining experiences:
- Celebrate significant occasions with personalized dining experiences onboard. The cruise staff can design exceptional dining events for you, whether it's a birthday, anniversary, or just a milestone in your journey.

10. Taking use of local markets:
- If your cruise schedule includes visits to local markets, browse the colorful booths offering fresh vegetables, artisan handicrafts, and regional specialties. It provides

a chance to engage with the culinary culture on a more intimate level.

Remember that dining on a Danube cruise is more than just food; it's an integral part of the whole experience. Allow your taste buds to become fellow passengers on this gastronomic journey down the Danube, whether you're enjoying a gourmet supper on deck, exploring onshore restaurants, or taking part in culinary activities.

Chapter 6. Itinerary Stops You'll Never Forget

Famous Cities and Towns

Vienna, Austria: A Cultural and Elegant Symphony.

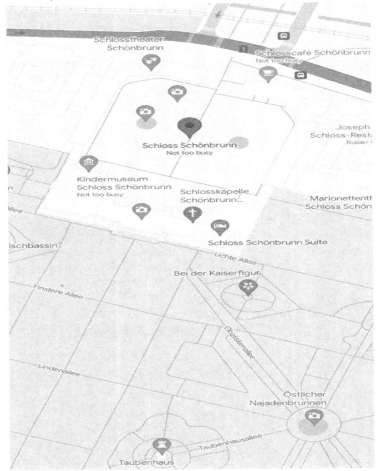

- Stepping into the Danube in Vienna was like entering a masterpiece. The city, which was a perfect blend of regal grandeur and creative attractiveness, left an indelible mark on my Danube River journey.

- As I went through the cobblestone pathways, I was captivated by the stunning combination of history and modernity. Vienna showed itself as a city in perpetual dialogue with its past and future, from the magnificent majesty of the Hofburg Palace to the contemporary pulse of the MuseumsQuartier.

Highlights:

1. Schloss Schönbrunn:
   - - The beauty of Schönbrunn Palace transported me back to the Habsburg era. The sumptuous apartments and immaculate gardens hummed with legends of imperial grandeur, offering a glimpse into royalty's lifestyle.

2. The Cathedral of Saint Stephen:
   - - The Gothic spires of St. Stephen's Cathedral stretched toward the sky. Inside, I was astounded by the stunning stained glass windows and the panoramic view from the South Tower.

3. The Belvedere Palace

- - The Belvedere Palace, a stunning example of Baroque architecture, housed an impressive collection of Austrian art. The famous Klimt paintings, particularly "The Kiss," added another layer of artistic brilliance to my stay in Vienna.

4. Coffee Shop Culture:
- - I spent languid days in historic cafés, immersed in Vienna's famed coffeehouse culture. Sipping a melange and eating Sachertorte were habits that helped me absorb the city's atmosphere.

5. State Opera of Vienna:
- - My favorite part of the vacation was an evening at the Vienna State Opera. The venue's timeless beauty, paired with a performance that mirrored the city's musical legacy, provided an unforgettable cultural experience.

6. Naschmarkt:
- - Naschmarkt, a busy market in Vienna that entices with a wide range of flavors. Exploring the market becomes a sensory journey via culinary delights, ranging from fresh vegetables to international delicacies.

7. MuseumsQuartier:
- - MuseumsQuartier, a cultural hub nestled in medieval courtyards and brimming with modern art galleries and elegant stores. The juxtaposition of contemporary inventiveness and old architecture represented Vienna's vibrant life.

- Every cobblestone in Vienna seemed to resound with Mozart's echoes and the beauty of the waltz. It was more than just a metropolis to me; it was a symphony of elegance and culture, beckoning me to waltz along its old streets and admire the timeless beauty of the Danube's banks.

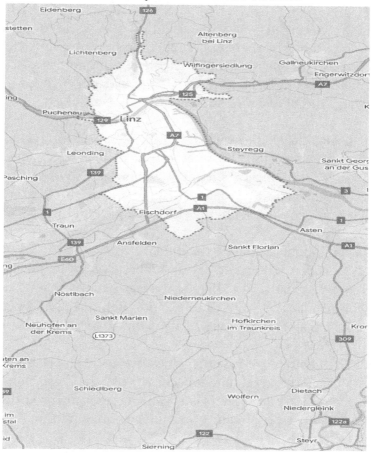

Linz, Austria: A Cultural Riverside Symphony.

As my Danube River cruise landed at Linz, Austria, I encountered a city that seamlessly blends historic beauty with modern vitality. The riverside scenery and the city's cultural highlights made for an unforgettable chapter in my travels.

Linz welcomed me with beautiful old-world houses along the riverbanks. While roaming around the cobblestone alleyways of Old Town, I came across lovely squares and appealing cafés where residents engaged in lively talks over coffee and pastries.

The Ars Electronica hub, a futuristic hub of interactive displays exploring the intersection of art, technology, and society, was a highlight of my Linz visit. The stunning modernity of this center created a stark yet harmonious contrast to the city's antique buildings.

The highlights of the city include:
1. Charms of Linz's Old Town: Walking about Linz's Old Town (Altstadt) was like entering a fairy tale. The vibrant façades of Gothic and Baroque buildings provided a breathtaking backdrop for exploration.

2. The Lentos Art Museum, which overlooks the Danube, has a remarkable collection of modern and contemporary art. The sleek glass façade mirrored the flow of the river, creating a striking contrast to the city's ancient core.

3. The Brucknerhaus Concert Hall is situated in Linz, a city with a long musical tradition. Even if you don't watch a play, the architecture and riverfront location make it a cultural landmark to see.

4. Linz Taste: Trying the local cuisine was a terrific experience. Linzer Torte, a classic Austrian delicacy, was a delicious treat, and typical Austrian coffee shops provided a pleasant setting to enjoy it.

5. Pöstlingberg City Views: I ascended Pöstlingberg by the renowned Linz Grotto Railway, which offers panoramic views of the city and the Danube. The exquisite pilgrimage church atop the hill added a historical element to the stunning setting.

Linz, with its blend of history and technology, soon became my favorite destination on my Danube journey. The city's commitment to maintaining its historic legacy while embracing modernity created an atmosphere in which I admired Austria's ability to combine the past and present.

Melk, Austria: A Danube Baroque Gem.
As the cruise liner approached the picturesque town of Melk, Austria, I found myself immersed in a scene right out of a fairytale. Melk is a baroque masterpiece nestled along the Danube's banks, and my visit here was nothing short of spectacular.

Highlights:

1. Melk monastery (Stift Melk): Melk's crown jewel is undeniably its majestic monastery perched on a hill above the town. As I reached the main staircase, I was met by the abbey's golden hues and stunning baroque architecture. The library, with its old texts and frescoes, transported me to an era of intellectual prosperity.

2. Melk's riverbank scenery is postcard-worthy. The beachfront is surrounded by lovely houses with flower-filled balconies, creating a tranquil environment for a stroll. Cafés along the river are great for sipping coffee while watching the Danube's peaceful currents.

3. Melk serves as the gateway to the Wachau Valley, a UNESCO World Heritage site famed for its vineyards and scenery. Melk's panoramic views of rolling hills and terraced vineyards are beautiful, providing a glimpse into Austria's rich splendor.

4. Local Flavors: Exploring Melk isn't complete unless you eat the local delicacies. I was able to enjoy apricot delights, a regional delicacy. The town's culinary products, ranging from apricot preserves to pastries, reflected the sweetness of its surroundings.

5. Markets and Town plaza: The town plaza is attractive, with its pastel-colored buildings and lively atmosphere. On market days, you'll find stalls brimming with fresh veggies, homemade crafts, and a vibrant display of local culture.

My fondest memory of Melk is standing in the abbey's courtyard, surrounded by centuries-old walls that echoed with history's whispers. The juxtaposition between the abbey's grandeur and the calm Danube landscape left an indelible effect on my journey. Melk exuded a timeless charm that made it a true highlight of my Danube River journey, whether strolling through the town's cobblestone lanes or gazing at the river from the abbey's terrace.

Dürnstein, Austria - A Danube Treasure

- Dürnstein, situated in the Wachau Valley, is a charming Austrian town that entices tourists with its medieval magnificence and breathtaking vistas. Dürnstein came as a lovely gem on my Danube River excursion, making an indelible impression on my holiday.

- When the cruise ship softly parked down the Danube, Dürnstein presented itself like a dream village. Cobblestone paths took me across town to the iconic blue and white church tower that dominates the skyline. The air was filled with the sweet perfume of flowering vines from nearby vineyards, creating a pleasing appearance.
- I wandered through the little alleyways, discovering centuries-old homes decorated with vibrant flowers. The town had a peaceful aura

that drew me to explore its history and enjoy its beauty.

Highlights:

1. Dürnstein Abbey: The town's center point is the Augustinian Abbey, a grand landmark dating back to the 15th century. The monastery's architecture, along with the tranquil courtyard, creates a serene environment.

2. The remnants of Kuenringer Castle, located on a hill above Dürnstein, provide panoramic views of the Danube Valley. The trek to the castle is rewarded with breathtaking vistas, making it a must-see.

3. Dürnstein is surrounded by vineyards and apricot orchards, adding to the region's reputation for wine and apricot goods. Tasting local wines and indulging in apricot delights was a highlight of my vacation.

4. Dürnstein is situated in the Wachau Valley, a UNESCO World Heritage Site known for its spectacular views. The vineyard-covered hills, flowing rivers, and historic towns create an enchanting panorama.

5. Artisan stores and cafés: The town's streets are packed with artisan shops selling local products and souvenirs. Outdoor cafés are great for savoring Austrian coffee and pastries while taking in the local environment.

Dürnstein appeared like a time capsule, with its timeless beauty and rich cultural heritage. It was a highlight of my Danube River vacation since it offered an excellent blend of history, natural beauty, and pleasant hospitality. As the sun set behind the hills, casting a warm glow over the settlement, I felt like I'd discovered a hidden jewel along the Danube's meandering path.

Budapest, Hungary: An Elegant and Historical Tapestry.

- Budapest emerged on the horizon as the Danube caressed our cruise ship, a city that effortlessly combines the grandeur of its past with the hectic pulse of modern life. When I strolled into the cobblestone streets, I was enveloped in a vivid symphony of culture, architecture, and real hospitality.

- Our journey began with a stroll over Budapest's renowned Chain Bridge, a testament to the city's architectural splendor. The city's lights illuminated the Danube as the sun sank, casting a stunning glow across the river. The view from the bridge included Buda Castle, which towered atop Castle Hill—a breathtaking spectacle that set the tone for our Budapest adventure.

- Ascending Castle Hill, we saw Fisherman's Bastion's colorful spires and terraces. The sweeping views of the city below were breathtaking, making an excellent backdrop for shots of Budapest's architectural treasures. Matthias Church, adjacent, stood as a timeless beauty, its dazzling tiles and Gothic spires telling stories from the past.

- A journey to Budapest would not be complete without a visit to the city's famed thermal baths. Gellért Baths, situated on the Buda side, provided a pleasant escape. As I submerged myself in the warm waves, I marveled at the surrounding Art Nouveau structures. Gellért Hill, crowned with the Liberty Statue, provided a postcard-worthy view of the city, capturing Budapest's blend of history and modernity.

- We explored the grandeur of Budapest's Andrássy Avenue, a UNESCO World Heritage site. The Hungarian State Opera House and the lovely mansions along the avenue were testaments to the city's prosperous past. The journey concluded in the Hungarian Parliament, a gleaming architectural masterpiece that reflects the city's political importance and commitment to democratic ideals.

- We strolled along the Danube Promenade as night fell, admiring the city's beauties in a soft light. The Parliament Building, Buda Castle, and bridges took on a new personality, exuding magic. We took a Danube night boat and glided under the brilliant lights, leaving memories of Budapest's magnificence on the canvas of the night sky.

- Budapest left an indelible mark on my Danube journey with its seamless blend of history, culture, and modern vibrancy. It was a city that spoke to my soul—a place where each turn revealed a new chapter in Hungary's rich history, inviting me to be a part of it.

Nuremberg, Germany: A Historical and Charming Tapestry.

- My visit to Nuremberg on my Danube River journey left an indelible impression, weaving together the threads of history, culture, and modern appeal. The city captivated me from the moment I stepped onto its cobblestone streets, with its medieval beauty and powerful character.

- Nuremberg is a living testament to Germany's rich heritage. The Imperial Castle, located on a hill, allows visitors to explore its well-preserved chambers and walk along centuries-old walls. As I wandered around the Old Town, the famed Nuremberg Castle and the towering Gothic façade of St. Lorenz Church transported me back in time.

- Nuremberg has played a significant part in modern history as the site of the Nuremberg hearings after World War II. The Palace of Justice, where the hearings were place, exudes solemnity. While in the courtroom where history occurred, I had a strong sense of thought about the pursuit of justice.

- Nuremberg's Market Square, or Hauptmarkt, is a vibrant hub where the city's heart beats the fastest. The Frauenkirche, with its majestic façade, and the famous Schöner Brunnen, a beautifully adorned fountain, provide the area's backdrop. During my visit, the market was bustling with stalls offering everything from local crafts to aromatic spices, making for a sensory feast.

- Nuremberg is famed for its culinary delights, and I couldn't pass up the local specialty, Nuremberg sausages. These delicious sausages became a gastronomic highlight, enjoyed in the magnificent setting of traditional beer gardens with sauerkraut and mustard.

- Nuremberg's renaissance extended beyond its old landmarks. The Documentation Center Nazi Party Rally Grounds provided a tough but essential examination of the city's involvement during the Nazi era. The museum's modern architecture symbolizes the city's commitment to face its complex history.

- In essence, Nuremberg is a city that perfectly combines the old with the contemporary, offering a diverse range of experiences to each visitor. Nuremberg is a multilayered jewel along the Danube that invites exploration, meditation, and a genuine appreciation for its tenacious character, from the echoes of the past behind its castle walls to the teeming energy of its markets.

Regensburg, Germany: A Historical River Tapestry.

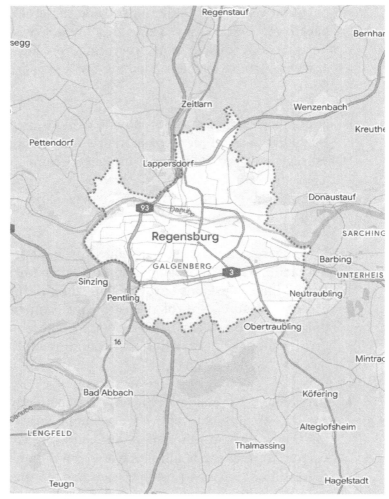

- Regensburg, perched on the Danube's banks, seemed to me like a fantasy hamlet, with each cobblestone street whispering tales of a bygone era. As I went around the city's well-preserved medieval heart, I was struck by its captivating blend of history and charm.

- Regensburg's heart is a UNESCO World Heritage site, and it's easy to see why. With its pointed spires and half-timbered houses, medieval architecture creates a timeless atmosphere. St. Peter's Cathedral, a Gothic masterpiece, commemorates the city's ecclesiastical heritage. Climbing the towers allowed for panoramic views of the river and the city's red-roofed skyline.

- As I crossed the famous Stone Bridge, I admired its history and beauty. This old bridge, adorned with sculptures and steeped in history, offers a beautiful vantage point for viewing the Danube's rushing waters. The river's tranquil currents reflected the evening sun's colors, casting a nice light over Regensburg's antique silhouette.

- Regensburg's attraction stems from its narrow lanes and hidden squares. Exploring these places took me to delightful cafés, artisan shops, and secret courtyards. The Haidplatz area, surrounded by colorful facades, was alive with the energy of both inhabitants and visitors enjoying the ambiance of this old marketplace.
- A visit to Regensburg would be completed without trying the city's culinary offerings. The city is known for its sausages, and I had the Regensburger Wurst, a local specialty, in the

historic Wurstkuchl. As I ate this delicious meal along the river, the aroma of cooked sausages wafted through the air.

- Regensburg combines its historical history with a vibrant cultural scene. Museums, galleries, and theaters are all examples of medieval architecture. Thurn und Taxis Palace, a historic royal residence, showcased the city's aristocratic background and offered a glimpse into bygone era opulence.

- Regensburg is, in essence, a living artwork in which the past and present intersect. Its beauty may be found not only in architectural wonders but also in the everyday rhythms of life that occur along the Danube. As I said farewell to this wonderful city, I carried not just memories of its attractions, but also a sense of having visited a living chapter in European history.

Passau, Germany - A Riverfront Treasure

- Passau, situated at the confluence of the Danube, Inn, and Ilz rivers, is a captivating city that blends history, culture, and natural beauty. Passau left an indelible impression on me, combining scenic cobblestone pathways, architectural marvels, and the soothing rhythm of flowing streams.

- Walking through Passau's Old Town seemed like returning to the past. The St. Stephen's Cathedral was a visual marvel, with its distinct baroque style and the world's largest cathedral organ. As I wandered the winding alleys, historic houses, and charming squares, each turn revealed a tale from the city's rich past.

- The convergence of the three rivers gave Passau a unique serenity. Riverside promenades were great for a stroll, allowing me to enjoy the serene views of the running streams and the lovely bridges that crossed the riverbanks. It was a place to relax, reflect, and enjoy the natural beauty that surrounded the city.

- Passau's commitment to the arts was evident in its vibrant cultural scene. The Glass Museum, which showcased intricate glasswork, and the contemporary galleries added a modern twist to the city's historic setting. I was able to attend a classical performance in the splendid chambers of the Bishop's Residence, which added to my enthusiasm for Passau's cultural riches.

- A boat trip along the Inn River offers a fresh viewpoint on Passau's magnificence. With each turn, the riverside view revealed itself, while the speaker provided historical context for the city. The Inn River's crystal-clear waters mirrored the city, creating a peaceful and stimulating atmosphere.

- Passau's culinary scene is enticing, with little cafés and diners tucked away in lovely corners. I enjoyed regional foods, drank coffee by the river, and tried Bavarian specialties. The gastronomy expedition mirrored the city's warm welcome and commitment to cultural preservation.

- Passau, in essence, enchanted me—a city where history whispers through cobblestone alleys, the Danube's embrace adds a rhythmic song, and ethnic blending creates a dynamic tapestry. Passau is a gem on the Danube, inviting visitors to immerse themselves in its timeless allure, whether by discovering its architectural treasures, enjoying local cuisine or just relaxing on the riverside.

Bratislava, Slovakia: The Danube's Whimsical Charm

Bratislava, perched along the Danube's banks, welcomed me with a blend of medieval grandeur and vibrant energy. As I explored the cobblestone streets and notable landmarks, the city revealed its individuality, making an indelible impression on my Danube trip.

Walking around the Old Town took me to a fairytale world. The lovely squares, pastel-colored cottages, and narrow lanes all contributed to a pleasant atmosphere.

The imposing presence of Bratislava Castle on a hill elevated the city's skyline.

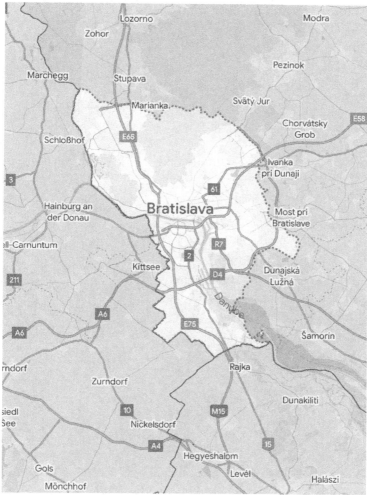

St. Michael's Gate, the only preserved medieval city gate, was one of the highlights. Climbing to the observation post gave me wonderful views of the Danube River and the surrounding region. The contrast between ancient architecture and modern metropolises was a visual feast.

As dusk set, I made my way to the SNP Bridge's UFO Observation Deck. The lights from the city reflected on the Danube, creating a wonderful ambiance. Bratislava's ability to seamlessly mix its rich history with modern, vibrant vitality impressed me here.

The highlights of the city include:

1. Explore Bratislava Castle, a spectacular fortress with a history dating back to the ninth century. The castle not only gives historical insights but also offers breathtaking views of the city and the river.

2. Old Town Square: Take a stroll around the gorgeous squares, which are alive with colorful buildings, outdoor cafes, and street performers. The Main Square, in particular, is a thriving hub of activity.

3. St. Martin's Cathedral: Admire the Gothic splendor of Bratislava's Saint Martin's Cathedral. Its tower dominates the skyline, and the inside is brimming with intriguing historical artifacts.

4. UFO Observation Deck: Take a once-in-a-lifetime trip to the top of the SNP Bridge for a breathtaking view of Bratislava. The UFO-shaped structure provides an excellent perspective of the city.

5. Bratislava City Museum: Learn about the city's history at the museum, which is located in the Old Town Hall. Exhibits portray the evolution of Bratislava from a medieval hamlet to a modern metropolis.

6. Devn Castle is located at the confluence of the Danube and Morava rivers, just a short sail from Bratislava. Its

remnants provide an interesting glimpse into the region's history.

Bratislava, with its distinctive architecture, rich history, and welcoming atmosphere, is a Danube treasure. My journey to this Slovakian city was an enthralling mixture of exploration and immersion in a culture that combines the past and present.

Off the Beaten Path Treasures.

Czech Republic:

esk Krumlov: The Bohemian Fairytale
esk Krumlov, situated in the beautiful South Bohemian region of the Czech Republic, is a picturesque hamlet that resembles a medieval fairy tale. Its historical value and well-preserved architecture make it a hidden gem worth discovering.

Highlights include:
1. esk Krumlov Castle: This UNESCO World Heritage site dominates the town's skyline and is a massive structure with Gothic, Renaissance, and Baroque influences. The castle offers stunning views of the Vltava River and the city underneath.

2. The Old Town Plaza is the pulsing heart of Esk Krumlov, a maze of narrow streets bordered by spectacular Renaissance and Baroque architecture.

Charming shops, cafés, and artisan boutiques add to the area's vibrant atmosphere.

3. Views of the Vltava River: A walk along the Vltava River, which flows through town, provides

postcard-worthy views. The ancient Moldau River Bridge and picturesque riverside houses add to the town's charming environment.

4. Visit the Eggenberg Brewery to learn about the local beer culture. Take a guided tour of the brewery to learn about the brewing process and enjoy classic Czech beers in a historical environment.

5. Egon Schiele Art Centrum in Esk Krumlov: Art enthusiasts may visit this center dedicated to the works of Egon Schiele, an Austrian painter associated with the Expressionist movement.

6. Rafting on the Vltava: Take a leisurely raft trip along the Vltava River to get a new perspective of Esk Krumlov. This leisure activity allows you to see the town's splendor from a new viewpoint.

7. Krumlov Mill: Nestled near the castle, Krumlov Mill is a wonderful location where you may enjoy a peaceful riverside environment and perhaps a meal or coffee.

8. esk Krumlov Puppet Museum: This unique museum has a collection of marionettes and puppetry-related antiquities, enabling visitors to experience the allure of traditional Czech puppetry.

esk Krumlov invites visitors to go back in time with its cobblestone streets, historic buildings, and sense of timelessness. Every facet of this Bohemian town tells a tale of history, art, and charm, whether you're strolling around the castle grounds or sipping coffee at a riverfront café.

Szentendre, Hungary: The Danube Art Enclave

Tourists are drawn to Szentendre, a charming town nestled along the Danube Bend, for its artistic appeal and vibrant environment. Szentendre is a living picture, with narrow cobblestone alleys leading to art galleries, charming cafés, and centuries-old structures.

Highlights:

1. Szentendre is regarded as a "museum town" because of its many museums and galleries. Visit the Margit Kovács Ceramic Museum and the Ferenczy Museum, both of which feature Hungarian art.

2. Baroque Churches: Explore the town's baroque structures, including the Blagovestenska Church and the Serbian Orthodox Church. Each building tells a story about Szentendre's many cultural influences.

3. Skansen Open-Air Museum: Step back in time to the Skansen Open-Air Museum, which depicts traditional Hungarian rural life. Historic features, such as a windmill and a press house, provide insight into rural culture.

4. Main Square (F tér) is Szentendre's heart, surrounded by pastel-colored buildings, artisan shops, and inviting cafés. It's a terrific area to soak in the atmosphere of the town.

5. Danube Promenade: Take a walk along the Danube Promenade to enjoy stunning views of the river and surrounding landscape. The riverfront offers a pleasant reprieve from the town's hectic streets.

6. Visit the Marzipan Museum to satiate your sweet tooth, where culinary art takes the form of stunning Marzipan sculptures. It's an enjoyable experience for both art and dessert lovers.

7. Kovács Margit Square is a haven for artists and art lovers. Browse through galleries showing a diverse selection of artworks, from paintings to sculptures, and you could find a one-of-a-kind piece to bring home.

Szentendre's distinct blend of creative vitality, cultural past, and riverfront allure marks it as a hidden gem along the Danube, beckoning tourists to wander its scenic streets and immerse themselves in the creativity that defines this wonderful Hungarian town.

Novi Sad, Serbia: The Danube Jewel
Novi Sad, situated on the Danube, is a cultural treasure that mixes history, vibrancy, and artistic beauty. Novi Sad, Serbia's second-largest city, invites tourists to

explore its rich history and participate in the lively atmosphere that marks this Danube destination.

Highlights include:

1. The Petrovaradin fortress, built in the 18th century, dominates the skyline and provides panoramic views of the city and the Danube. The fortress, which includes the iconic clock tower, hosts cultural events like the well-known EXIT music festival.

2. Old Town and Dunavska Street: Wander through the Old Town's narrow streets, where Baroque architecture meets bohemian flair. Dunavska Street, lined with cafés and shops, is perfect for a stroll.

3. Admire the stunning architecture of this Orthodox church, known for its intricate murals and majestic dome. The church commemorates Novi Sad's religious and cultural past.

4. Dunavski Park: This lovely green oasis is perfect for a peaceful day. The park has sculptures, fountains, and pathways, making it a calm oasis in the heart of the city.

5. Danube Promenade: Take in the riverfront beauty while walking along the Danube Promenade. Take in the landscape, visit riverside cafés, and soak in the lively atmosphere.

6. Museum of Vojvodina: This museum, housed in a spectacular 18th-century baroque architecture, teaches visitors about the local history. The shows include artifacts from ancient times to the present.

7. Svetozar Miletic Square: The central square, surrounded by excellent architecture including the neo-Renaissance City Hall, is a hub of activity. It serves as a gathering place for events and gatherings, as well as an excellent starting point for exploring the city.

Novi Sad, sometimes known as the "Athens of Serbia," is a city where history and modernity coexist. Novi Sad enchants tourists with its many attractions along the Danube, ranging from historic monuments to beautiful riverfront views.

Veliko Tarnovo, Bulgaria: The Bulgarian History Citadel Veliko Tarnovo, set on the Yantra River, rises like a medieval masterpiece, telling tales about Bulgaria's rich history. This often-overlooked hidden gem offers a captivating blend of architectural wonders, breathtaking landscape, and a vibrant cultural atmosphere.

Highlights include:

1. Tsarevets Fortress: Veliko Tarnovo, capped by the magnificent Tsarevets Fortress, invites visitors to go back in time. The fortress atop a hill not only provides panoramic views of the city but also houses historic structures such as the Patriarchal Cathedral.

2. Samovodska Charshia: Take a stroll through the cobblestone streets of Samovodska Charshia, an artisan's area that has preserved its 19th-century charm. Traditional workshops, shops, and restaurants showcase Bulgaria's craftsmanship and kindness.

3. Admire the majestic Asen's Monument, a symbol of the medieval Asen dynasty. It is located on a hill and offers a unique perspective of Veliko Tarnovo's picturesque surroundings.

4. Tsarevets Fortress's mesmerizing Sound and Light Show brings the city's history to life with vivid illuminations, music, and narration.

5. Gurko Street: Stroll along Gurko Street, which is dotted with colorful homes and provides a nostalgic glimpse into Veliko Tarnovo's architectural history.

6. Visit architectural reserves like Arbanasi, which has well-preserved buildings and churches that represent the region's Renaissance beauty.

Veliko Tarnovo, with its hilltop castles, winding alleyways, and unique feeling of antiquity, is a hidden treasure worth discovering for anybody searching for a Bulgarian experience.

Iron Gates: The Majestic Danube Gorge.

The Iron Gates is a breathtaking natural wonder situated on the Danube River, dividing Serbia and Romania. This lovely canyon carved through the Carpathian Mountains is a hidden gem with breathtaking views and historical significance.

Highlights include:

1. The Iron Gates Canyon, a geological wonder, has towering limestone cliffs that rise abruptly from the river. As the Danube runs down the narrow route, the sheer size of the canyon creates a breathtaking image.
2. Decebalus Statue: Take admire the massive rock sculpture of Decebalus, Dacia's penultimate monarch. This massive sculpture cut into the rock adds a feeling of historic history to the landscape.

3. Tabula Traiana: A Roman monument may be seen on the Serbian side of the canyon. This marble plaque commemorates the building of a Roman highway and sheds light on the region's historical relationships.

4. A Danube River cruise via the Iron Gates offers a front-row view of this natural wonder. The journey takes passengers down the canyon's narrowest and most spectacular stretch, allowing them to soak in the stunning surroundings.

5. Natural Reserves: The Iron Gates region is abundant in plants and animals. Nature enthusiasts will appreciate

the untouched wilderness of Serbia's Djerdap National Park and Romania's Iron Gates Natural Park.

6. Rural towns: Along the Danube's banks, you'll find charming communities where time seems to stand still. These hidden towns provide a glimpse into traditional living in this remote yet beautiful corner of Europe.

The Iron Gates, with their stunning blend of natural beauty and historical remains, enable tourists to deviate from the main path and see a less-explored element of the Danube's magnificent journey.

Castle Heights and Riverside Tranquility, Visegrád, Hungary.

Visegrád, situated in the Danube Bend, is a charming Hungarian treasure that blends history, natural beauty, and cultural interest.

Highlights:

1. Visegrád Castle: Perched on a hill, the medieval Visegrád Castle offers stunning views of the Danube. Explore the medieval ruins, which include the famed Solomon Tower.

2. The remains of the Royal Palace of Visegrád exhibit the grandeur of Hungary's medieval aristocracy. Wander

the medieval walls, recalling the regal history that previously flourished there.

3. Danube Bend Views: Visegrád's scenic beauty extends beyond its historical sites. The Danube Bend runs underneath the town, providing a beautiful backdrop for its landmarks.

4. Solomon's Tower: A trek to the castle complex's Solomon's Tower provides breathtaking views of the surrounding region. It's an excellent spot for capturing the essence of the Danube's meandering flow.

5. Visegrád Citadel: Explore the Visegrád Citadel by plunging into the riverbank. This fortress, situated in a magnificent natural setting, offers a private getaway with riverfront walks and serene views.

6. The Royal Residence Museum explores Hungary's royal history via exhibitions that depict the lives of medieval kings and queens who once decorated Visegrád.

7. The Esztergom Basilica, Hungary's largest church, is just a short distance away and beckons with its stunning architecture and cultural significance.

Visegrád, with its historic interest and natural beauty, is a hidden gem along the Danube—a place where the river's timeless flow meets remnants of Hungary's royal history.

Onboard Experience

Themed Gala Nights: Elegance and Entertainment Afloat.
Themed Gala Nights on a Danube River cruise provide a sense of grandeur and excitement to the onboard experience. These unique evenings are intended to transport visitors into a world of luxury, entertainment, and cultural enrichment.

Key Elements:

- Dress Code: Themed Gala Nights may have a particular dress code that encourages passengers to wear stunning attire inspired by the chosen theme. Whether it's a black-tie dinner or a costume party, tourists may show off their style.

- Fine Dining: Gala Nights are enhanced by extraordinary dining experiences. The ship's culinary team creates bespoke meals, including gourmet delights, to enhance the event with culinary excellence.

- Themed Gala Nights provide a variety of entertainment options, including live music performances and dance acts. Professional artists may take the stage, providing passengers with an excellent experience as they enjoy the night's festivities.

- Decor and Ambiance: The inside of the ship is transformed to fit the evening's theme. Lavish décor, ambient lighting, and painstakingly picked details create an immersive environment that transports visitors to a magical dimension.

- Cultural Immersion: Themed Gala Nights usually include elements of local culture or cultural sites from the cruise itinerary. This helps tourists feel more connected to the places they visit.

- Photography Opportunities: Passengers may capture the magic of the evening with onboard photography facilities. The ship's photographers may provide professional photo sessions, providing visitors with lasting memories of the stunning event.

Whether it's a traditional masquerade, a celebration of local traditions, or a nod to the elegance of a bygone era, Themed Gala Nights on a Danube River cruise bring an extra layer of charm to the journey, providing one-of-a-kind experiences for everyone aboard.

Onboard Entertainment Shows: An Exciting Cruise Experience

On a Danube River cruise, onboard entertainment presentations enliven your journey with captivating performances that combine culture, music, and storytelling. These performances are intended to improve your evenings and create a pleasant environment while you sail along the ancient river.

Key features:

- Enjoy a diverse range of entertainment, from live music and dancing to dramatic performances. The onboard entertainment caters to a wide range of tastes, so there's something for everyone.

- Cultural Showcases: Immerse yourself in the many cultures along the Danube with performances of local folklore, traditional music, and dance. These cultural exhibits explore the artistic heritage of the places you visit.

- Live music events include genres such as classical, jazz, and folk. Talented painters often beautify the onboard stages, providing a magnificent background for your trip.

- Interactive performances encourage audience participation, transforming the performance into an immersive experience. Whether it's a dance class or a comedy night, these participation elements create great memories.

- Professional entertainers, such as magicians and comedians, dancing troupes, and solo musicians, are often featured aboard cruise ships. These artists bring a high level of experience and originality to the boardroom stage.

- Enjoy theatrical productions such as themed plays, musicals, and adaptations of local tales. These performances transport you to other eras and tales, enriching the cultural journey.

- Dinner Entertainment: Some cruises provide entertainment during the meal, enhancing your dining experience with live music, small ensembles, or exclusive performances that set a sophisticated tone.

- Onboard entertainment concerts are an exciting part of your Danube River cruise, adding flair to your evenings and ensuring that every moment spent on the ship is packed with enchantment, cultural immersion, and the excitement of live performances.

- Wine-tasting sessions onboard provide a nice tour through the vineyards along the Danube. Whether you're a seasoned oenophile or a casual wine enthusiast, these seminars provide a unique opportunity to sample the tastes of the areas you visit.

- Wine tastings, which are often organized by trained sommeliers or local experts, delve into the complexities of regional varietals while also sharing tales about the vineyards and the winemaking process. Participants will sample a variety of wines, ranging from crisp whites to bold reds, each exhibiting the terroir of the Danube Valley.

- As you swirl, smell, and taste, you will not only enjoy the sensuous pleasures of wine but also learn about the cultural and historical significance of winemaking along the Danube. It's a social and educational experience that helps you connect more deeply with the places you visit, one glass at a time.

Fitness Classes on Board: Energize Your Danube Journey

Onboard exercise sessions will keep you active and energetic during your Danube River trip. These programs are designed to appeal to a wide range of fitness levels, allowing you to maintain your health while enjoying the beautiful surroundings along the river.

Key features:

- Guided activities: Join expert fitness instructors for a variety of guided exercises such as aerobics, yoga, and resistance training. These programs are designed to accommodate a wide range of fitness levels, from beginners to advanced athletes.

- Scenic Exercise Locations: Many river cruise ships include outside areas, such as sundecks, where exercise sessions are conducted. Exercising against the backdrop of the Danube's beautiful surroundings adds an element of enjoyment to your workout.

- Wellness Programs: Some cruises provide holistic wellness programs that include fitness and mindfulness. To start your day on a positive note, try morning yoga or meditation courses.

- Group Dynamics: Fitness activities on board can foster a sense of community among other travelers. Group exercises provide a social and motivational aspect, resulting in a pleasant and engaging experience.

- Varying Class Options: Whether you prefer low-impact activities like stretching or high-energy workouts, cruise fitness programs often provide a variety of options. Choose classes that match your workout goals and preferences.

- Flexible Schedule: Cruise fitness programs often include flexible schedules, allowing you to participate at times that suit your everyday schedule. Everyone has an option, whether it's early morning yoga or afternoon aerobics class.

Benefits:

- Health Integration: Fitness programs enhance your overall health experience, complementing the holistic approach used by many river cruise operators.
- Stress Reduction: Exercise is an excellent stress reducer. Among the cultural excursions and sightseeing, fitness classes provide a focused time for physical activity and relaxation.
- Individual Attention: Instructors often provide individual attention to ensure that participants maintain proper technique and get the most out of their workout.
- Whether you're a fitness fanatic or just want to add some exercise to your cruise itinerary,

onboard fitness classes provide a balanced and enjoyable method to stay active while cruising the Danube.

Interactions with locals

Engaging with locals along the Danube is an enriching aspect of the river cruise experience, providing a real glimpse into the heart and spirit of each town. Here are some of the ways you may form significant connections with the people who live on the Danube's beaches:

1. Marketplace Banter:
   - - Wander through busy local markets, where the vibrant tapestry of colors and smells provides a background for lively conversations with vendors. Try your hand at a few local phrases, and you could find yourself sharing tales about your favorite local items.

2. Riverside Conversations:
   - - Take a stroll along the riverbanks and strike up conversations with inhabitants who like the outdoors. Whether it's a simple chat with a fisherman casting their lines or a discussion on the area's rich history, these exchanges provide a genuine glimpse into ordinary life.

3. Culinary Connections:

- - Take a cooking class or dine at a local restaurant, where the welcoming atmosphere often extends beyond the meal. Conversations with chefs, restaurant owners, and other customers may provide valuable information about culinary traditions and local preferences.

4. Folklore Performances:
   - - Attend local folklore performances, where traditional music and dance unite communities. Don't be afraid to join in the festivities, whether it's a dance or just clapping along to the rhythm.

5. Artisan workshops:
   - - Visit artisan workshops and engage with craftsmen who are preserving traditional skills. Learn about their crafts, ask questions, and even try your hand at creating something unique to the region.

6. Cultural Events:
   - - Attend local events, festivals, or cultural gatherings to immerse oneself in the community environment. Participate in rituals, witness performances, and enjoy the great moments that local festivals provide.

7. Historical narratives:
   - - When visiting historical sites or museums, strike up conversations with local guides or historians. Their stories often go beyond facts

and statistics, adding personal experiences that provide a greater understanding of the region's history.

8. Language Exchange:
- • - Don't be afraid to attempt the local language. Even simple statements communicate respect and openness, which typically prompts people to smile and eagerly share their cultural traditions.

- • These interactions with Danube inhabitants enrich your travel experience, creating lasting memories that extend beyond the river's physical majesty and surroundings. These connections with locals, whether via shared humor, cultural insights, or meaningful conversations, are an important part of the Danube's appeal.

Cruise Ship Accommodations: Sail in Comfort and Style

Cruise ship accommodations along the Danube provide a variety of options, so that visitors may pick a peaceful refuge adapted to their preferences. Prices may vary based on the cabin type, cruise company, and specific features. Here's a look at the accommodation kinds you could encounter:

1. Interior Cabins:
   - - Price range: $1,000–$2,500.
   - - These accommodations, located within the ship, offer comfortable lodgings with all necessary amenities. They provide a cost-effective option for travelers who prefer the cruise experience over expansive in-cabin views.

2. Ocean View Cabins:
   - - Price Range: $1,500 to $3,500.
   - - Ocean View rooms offer windows or portholes, allowing travelers to enjoy beautiful views of the Danube directly from their cabins. Prices vary according to cabin size and location.

3. Balcony Cabins:

- - Prices range from $2,500 to $5,000.
- - Balcony accommodations provide their own outside space, allowing guests to enjoy the fresh air and breathtaking views. The price range varies according to the cruise company, cabin size, and itinerary.

4. Suites:
- - Price range: $4,000–$10,000+
- - Suites provide bigger accommodations with separate living areas, extra amenities, and, in certain cases, unique incentives. Prices vary substantially based on the level of luxury and cruise line.

5. Luxury suites and staterooms:
- - Price Range: $8,000 to $20,000+
- - For visitors seeking the ultimate in luxury, cruise lines may provide top-tier suites complete with premium amenities, private butlers, and exclusive perks. The range may widen depending on the level of luxury.

6. Single cabins:
- - Price range: $1,500 to $4,000.
- - Cruise lines often offer single rooms for lone travelers, which is a nice and cost-effective option. Prices may vary based on the cruise operator and the amenities provided.

7. Family cabins:

- - Price range: $3,000 to $7,000.
- - Family cabins accommodate larger groups by offering interconnected rooms or dedicated family suites. Prices vary depending on the cruise line, stateroom configuration, and amenities provided to families.

- It is important to note that these cost ranges may alter based on cruise company offers, the time of booking, and unique itineraries. Additionally, river cruises on the Danube may have distinct pricing dynamics than ocean cruises. Always check with the cruise operator for the most up-to-date pricing information based on your preferences and travel dates.

Onshore Hotels and Lodgings

General overview of hotels along the Danube

1. Luxury Hotels (about $200 or more per night):
   - Hotel Sacher Vienna (Vienna, Austria): This iconic hotel, located near the State Opera, is known for its sumptuous rooms and the famous Sachertorte.

   - Four Seasons Hotel Gresham Palace (Budapest, Hungary): This Art Nouveau treasure on the Danube offers beautiful suites and breathtaking views of the Chain Bridge.

2. Mid-range hotels (about $100 to $200 per night)

- NH Collection Nürnberg City (Nuremberg, Germany): A modern hotel in the city of Nuremberg that offers comfort and convenience at mid-range prices.

- Austria Trend Hotel Schloss Dürnstein (Dürnstein, Austria): Located in the Wachau Valley, this charming hotel combines tradition with contemporary amenities.

3. Budget-Friendly Options (Under $100/Night):

- Hotel Gat Point Charlie (Bratislava, Slovakia): A low-cost hotel in the ancient city center that offers a comfortable stay without breaking the bank.

- Easyhotel Budapest Oktogon (Budapest, Hungary): An affordable option in Budapest that offers simplicity and convenience to budget-conscious travelers.

Chapter 9. Practical Travel Tips

Packing Essentials

Taking a Danube River cruise allows you to admire the beauty of European landmarks while floating along one of the continent's most famous rivers. To ensure a comfortable and enjoyable trip, consider taking the following essentials:

1. Clothing: -
   - Casual wear for daytime outings, such as lightweight shirts, shorts, or skirts.
   - Formal Attire: Bring a few semi-formal outfits for board dinners or special events.
   - Layers: Pack a light jacket or sweater for cold evenings, especially if you're traveling in the spring or fall.
   - Rain Gear: If it rains unexpectedly, a waterproof jacket or travel umbrella might come in handy.

2. Footwear:
   - Sneakers or comfortable walking shoes are recommended for exploring cobblestone streets and historical sites.
   - Dress Shoes: Pack a pair of dressier shoes for formal occasions or dining onboard.

3. Accessories:

- Sun Protection: Sunglasses, wide-brimmed hats, and sunscreen to protect against the European sun while onshore activities.

Daypack:

- A small daypack is great for carrying essential items on trips.
- Travel Adapters: Make sure you have the right power adapters for the countries you'll be visiting to charge your electronics.

4. Travel Documents:

- Passport and Visa: Make sure your passport is valid for at least six months beyond your planned trip. Check the visa requirements for the countries to which you want to visit.
- Travel Insurance: Bring proof of your travel insurance coverage.
- Cruise Documents: Include your cruise itinerary, tickets, and any applicable reservation confirmations.

5. Health and Medicine:

- Prescription Medications: Bring enough for the duration of your trip, along with a copy of your prescription.
- Basic First Aid Kit: Include items like pain relievers, bandages, and any personal medications.

6. Technology and Entertainment:

- Camera: Capture the stunning views along the Danube. Don't forget about extra memory cards and charging supplies.
- E-Reader or Books: Spend some time reading during your leisure.
- Adapter and Chargers: Bring chargers for your devices and make sure they are compatible with European outlets.

7. Pack travel-sized toiletries, including shampoo, conditioner, toothbrush, and other personal care items.
- Wet wipes or hand sanitizer: Great for quick cleanups on vacations.

8. Money and Security: - Be sure to notify your bank of your vacation dates and bring local currency for small purchases.
- Money Belt or Neck Bag: Consider using a secure bag to protect valuables on trips.

9. Miscellaneous:
- Travel Pillow: Provides comfort during long journeys or relaxation on a ship.
- Reusable Water Bottle: Stay hydrated during your vacation.
- Collapsible Tote Bag: Perfect for carrying souvenirs or other items purchased on your vacation.

10. Snorkeling Gear:

- Bring a snorkel, mask, and fins if your cruise itinerary includes snorkeling stops.

Remember to tailor your packing list to the specific season, activities, and destinations included in your Danube River cruise itinerary. Additionally, check with your cruise line for any unique dress codes or recommended items based on their services and activities.

Language Tips and Common Phrases for Danube Destinations

Embracing the local languages along the Danube enriches your cultural experience. While English is often spoken in tourist areas, attempting to communicate in the local language may foster ties. Here are some linguistic pointers and frequent terms from several Danube destinations:

1. Austria/Germany: - Hello: Hello, Thank you: Thank you - goodbye. Excuse me: Auf Wiedersehen Entschuldigung
- Yes or No: Ja/Nein

2. Hungarian (Hungary).
- Hello: Szia (casual); Jó napot (formal).
- Thank you. Köszönöm

- Goodbye. Viszlát apologizes: Please choose Yes or No. Igen/Nem

3. Slovak (Slovakia).
- Hello: Ahoj: Thank you. Ďakujem: Goodbye Dovidenia: Excuse me. Prepare: Yes/No. Áno/Nie

4. Serbian (Serbia).
- Hello: Zdravo – Thank you! Hvala
- Goodbye. Doviđenja: Excuse me. Introducing Izvinite. Yes/No: Da/Ne

5. Romanian (Romania).
- Hello: Thank you. Mulţumesc
- Goodbye. Excuse me: Scuzaţi-mi.
- Yes/No: Da/Nu

6. Bulgarian (Bulgaria).
Hello: Здравейте (Zdraveyte). Thank you: Congratulations (Blagodarya).
- Goodbye. Dovizhdane - Excuse me. Извинете (Izvinete
- Yes or No: Да/Не (Da/Ne)

7. Croatian (Croatia).
- Hello: Bok - Thank you! Hvala
- Goodbye. Doviđenja: Excuse me. Optional: Yes/No Da/Ne

8. Czech (Czech Republic)
- Hello: Ahoj: Thank you. Thank you and goodbye. Excuse me. Proposal: Yes/No. Ano/Ne

Language tip: Greet with a genuine smile, which is frequently recognized and liked.

Learn basic numbers, which are especially useful for transactions and directions.

Polite phrases such as "please" and "thank you" are useful in every language.

Practice Pronunciation: Even if your pronunciation isn't perfect, locals will appreciate it.

Remember that striving to learn the local language, no matter how basic, shows respect and usually leads to more meaningful interactions on your Danube River cruise.

Currency Tips and Local Currencies on the Danube River.

While traveling down the Danube River, you will see a variety of currencies. Here is monetary guidance and an overview of local currencies for various major destinations:

1. Euro (€) is used in Austria, Slovakia, and Germany.
- Currency Tips: Euros are widely accepted, and you may withdraw them from ATMs in these countries. Inform your bank of your travel dates to avoid any issues with card transactions.

2. Hungarian Forint (HUF) is used in Hungary.

- Money Tips: Exchange money before you arrive, or withdraw Hungarian Forints at local ATMs. Major credit cards are often accepted, however, taking cash to smaller establishments is vital.

3. Czech Koruna (CZK) is used in the Czech Republic. Currency Tips: Currency exchange agencies are common in tourist areas. Credit cards are widely accepted, although having some local currency for small purchases is essential.

4. Croatian Kuna (HRK) is a currency used in Croatia, particularly while traveling along the Danube.
- currencies Exchange currencies at banks or currency exchange offices. Credit cards are accepted in larger establishments, however cash may be preferred at smaller locations.

5. Serbian Dinar (RSD): - Currency in Serbia. currencies Exchange Tips: Visit a local bank or exchange bureau to exchange currencies. Credit cards are accepted in major cities, although carrying cash is essential in rural areas.

6. Bulgarian Lev (BGN): - Currency in Bulgaria. Currency tips: Banks and currency exchange bureaus are where you may exchange currencies. Credit cards are widely accepted in large cities, however cash may be preferred in smaller towns and rural areas.

7. Romanian Leu (RON): - Currency in Romania. Currency tips: Banks and exchange bureaus are where

you may exchange currencies. Credit cards are widely accepted in urban areas, however cash is recommended for rural locations.

8. Euro (€) - Used in Slovakia and Germany.
- Currency tips: Similar to Austria, Euros are widely recognized in Slovakia and Germany. ATMs allow for withdrawals in local currencies.

General Currency Tips:

- Currency Exchange Locations: To ensure fair pricing, exchange currencies at official exchange offices or banks.
- ATM Withdrawals: ATMs are often found in urban areas. Inform your bank about your travel dates to avoid any issues with card transactions.

- Tiny Denominations: Reserve tiny denominations for gratuities, local markets, and small purchases. Larger bills may not be accepted everywhere.

- Check Currency Symbols: Be aware of currency symbols to avoid misunderstandings, especially while using various currencies nearby.

Remember that money use varies by country, so it's a good idea to bring both cash and credit cards.

For Smartphone and Digital Camera Users:

1. Use soft, warm light during the golden hours (early morning or late afternoon) to create beautiful scenes. This lighting enhances the colors and adds a beautiful touch to your photographs.

2. Focus on Composition: - Use basic composition ideas, such as the rule of thirds. Place large objects, such as rivers, bridges, or castles, along these lines to create visually appealing images.

3. Capture Reflections: - Use the Danube's beautiful surface to capture stunning reflections. Calm waters early in the morning or around nightfall provide excellent conditions.

4. Experiment with Angles: - Try different views to get a fresh perspective on familiar events. Take low-angle photos to get a new view of the riverbanks and buildings.

5. Include foreground elements: Incorporate interesting foreground elements to provide depth and character to your photographs. This might be river stones, flowers, or architectural components.

6. Zoom with Your Feet: - Instead of relying only on digital zoom, physically approach your subject. This protects image quality and results in clearer photos.

7. Use HDR Mode: The High Dynamic Range (HDR) option balances exposure in challenging lighting conditions. It's particularly useful for photographing landscapes with both bright skies and gloomy areas.

For smartphone users:

8. Tap to focus and adjust exposure: - To manage your smartphone's camera, tap the screen to choose focus and exposure. This guarantees that the key topic is clearly defined and that the exposure is balanced.

9. Use Panorama Mode: Use your smartphone's panorama feature to capture the vast Danube River. Slowly pan over the subject to get broad landscape photographs.

10. Experiment with Camera Apps: - Try third-party camera apps with manual controls. This allows you to adjust settings such as ISO and shutter speed for more creative freedom.

For Digital Camera Users:

11. Use RAW format when supported by your camera. This gives you more flexibility in post-processing, allowing you to increase details and colors.

12. Manual Mode for Control: - Adjust aperture, shutter speed, and ISO using manual settings. This is especially critical when dealing with difficult lighting conditions.

13. Use a Tripod: - A little portable tripod may stabilize your camera and prevent blurry photos in low light or lengthy exposures.

Remember that the most important aspect of photography is to have fun and capture moments that resonate with you. Experiment with these approaches to acquire your own perspective on the beautiful scenery along the Danube.

Websites and helpful contacts

Here are some useful websites and information that might enhance your Danube River cruise experience:

1. Cruise Line: - [Viking River Cruises].(https://www.vikingrivercruises.com/)
- AmaWaterways (https://www.amawaterways.com/)
[Uniworld Boutique River Cruises](https://www.uniworld.com/)
- Avalon Waterways (https://www.avalonwaterways.com/)
- Emerald Waterways (https://www.emeraldwaterways.com/)

2. Currency Exchange and Conversion: [XE Currency Converter](https://www.xe.com/currencyconverter/).
-       [OANDA   Currency   Converter] (https://www.oanda.com/currency/converter/).

3. Local Tourism Boards: - Austria Tourism Board (https://www.austria.info/).
-       [Hungary   Tourism   Board] (https://visithungary.com/).
-       [Germany   National   Tourist   Board] (https://www.germany.travel/en).
The   [Slovakia   Tourism Board](https://slovakia.travel/en)
-       [The   Serbian   Tourist Organization](http://www.serbia.travel/)
- [Bulgaria Tourism] (https://bulgariatravel.org/en/).
- [Romanian Tourism](http://romaniatourism.com/)

4.   Language   Learning   Apps: - [Duolingo].(https://www.duolingo.com/)
- [babbel](https://www.babbel.com/)
[Memrise](https://www.memrise.com/)

5. Health and Safety: - [CDC - Travel Health Notices](https://wwwnc.cdc.gov/travel/notices).   - [World   Health   Organization   (WHO)]. (https://www.who.int/)

6. Local Emergency Contacts: - Emergency services: 112 (universal emergency number in the European Union) -

Local emergency numbers may differ by country, so be prepared with specific numbers for each visit.

7. BBC Weather - Danube Region weather forecast. (https://www.bbc.com/weather)

8. Transportation: - Eurolines (International Bus Service)(https://www.eurolines.com/)
-        [Eurail: European   Train Travel](https://www.eurail.com/)

9. Check local tourism websites for upcoming activities and festivals during your visit.

Always check and examine the most recent information before your trip, and feel free to explore additional resources based on your specific interests and needs. Safe travels!

Printed in Great Britain
by Amazon